Ternus, Lynn
Nebraska

CORE LIBRARY OF US STATES

Nebraska

BY LYNN TERNUS

CONTENT CONSULTANT
Emily Osberg-Brown
Education Supervisor
University of Nebraska State Museum

Core Library
An Imprint of Abdo Publishing
abdobooks.com

abdobooks.com

Published by Abdo Publishing, a division of ABDO, PO Box 398166, Minneapolis, Minnesota 55439. Copyright © 2023 by Abdo Consulting Group, Inc. International copyrights reserved in all countries. No part of this book may be reproduced in any form without written permission from the publisher. Core Library™ is a trademark and logo of Abdo Publishing.

Printed in the United States of America, North Mankato, Minnesota.
052022
092022

Cover Photos: Shutterstock Images, map and icons, goldenrod
Interior Photos: Zack Frank/Shutterstock Images, 4–5; Mihai Andritoiu/Shutterstock Images, 8, 45; Red Line Editorial, 9 (Nebraska), 9 (USA); Shutterstock Images, 10; Jim West/Alamy, 12–13, 43; Mare Kuliasz/Shutterstock Images, 15, 22–23; Lukasz Stefanski/Shutterstock Images, 18 (flag); David Spates/Shutterstock Images, 18 (bird); Arunee Rodloy/Shutterstock Images, 18 (fish); Lutsenko Larissa/Shutterstock Images, 18 (flower); Tom Reichner/Shutterstock Images, 18 (deer), 27; Weldon Schloneger/Shutterstock Images, 30–31; The Color Archives/Alamy, 33; Shannon Ramos/EyeEm/Getty Images, 36–37; Jerry Mennenga/Zuma Press/Newscom, 40

Editor: Marie Pearson
Series Designer: Joshua Olson

Library of Congress Control Number: 2021951412

Publisher's Cataloging-in-Publication Data

Names: Ternus, Lynn, author.
Title: Nebraska / by Lynn Ternus
Description: Minneapolis, Minnesota : Abdo Publishing, 2023 | Series: Core library of US states | Includes online resources and index.
Identifiers: ISBN 9781532197680 (lib. bdg.) | ISBN 9781098270445 (ebook)
Subjects: LCSH: U.S. states--Juvenile literature. | Midwest States--Juvenile literature. | Nebraska--History--Juvenile literature. | Physical geography--United States--Juvenile literature.
Classification: DDC 978.2--dc23

Population demographics broken down by race and ethnicity come from the 2019 census estimate. Population totals come from the 2020 census.

CONTENTS

CHAPTER ONE
The Cornhusker State 4

CHAPTER TWO
History of Nebraska 12

CHAPTER THREE
Geography and Climate 22

CHAPTER FOUR
Resources and Economy 30

CHAPTER FIVE
People and Places 36

Important Dates. 42

Stop and Think. 44

Glossary. 46

Online Resources 47

Learn More 47

Index 48

About the Author. 48

CHAPTER ONE

THE CORNHUSKER STATE

A group of people hop on their bikes and head down a paved path. They pedal along Prairie View Trail to see giant rock formations at Scotts Bluff National Monument. This area in Nebraska is protected by the federal government. It contains 3,000 acres (1,200 ha) of land in the western part of the state. Visitors can see tall prairie grasses blowing in the Nebraska breeze. They can also see the area's rocky badlands and soaring bluffs.

Scotts Bluff National Monument is in western Nebraska.

Beyond the big cities in eastern Nebraska lie huge fields and prairies. Tractors harvest gold-tasseled corn. Nebraska is one of the biggest corn producers in the country. Because of this, its nickname is the Cornhusker State. A cornhusker is a person or machine that separates an ear of corn from its husk.

ABOUT NEBRASKA

Nebraska is part of the Midwest region of the United States. It is near the center of the country. Nebraska shares a border with six other states. Colorado and Wyoming lie to the west. South Dakota borders it to the north. Iowa and

AN IMPORTANT LANDMARK

The rock formations at Scotts Bluff National Monument reach toward the blue sky. The bluff has important history. For centuries American Indians lived in the area. The Sioux, Cheyenne, and Arapaho peoples hunted bison there. When white settlers came in the 1840s and 1850s, they used the bluff as a landmark. It helped them navigate the Oregon and California Trails on the journey west.

Missouri lie to the east. Kansas borders Nebraska to the south. The Missouri River is the second-longest river in the United States. It forms some of Nebraska's borders with South Dakota, Iowa, and Missouri.

Most people in Nebraska live in the eastern part of the state, near the Missouri and Platte Rivers. Omaha is Nebraska's biggest city. It's along the Missouri River. Large companies have offices in this city.

PERSPECTIVES
MOVING TO THE COUNTRY

Steph Larsen used to live in Washington, DC, but accepted a job offer in Nebraska. Her friends were shocked when she told them she was moving. They couldn't understand why Larsen would want to leave a big city to live in rural Nebraska. But Larsen had a different view. She was tired of the large crowds in DC. She felt like the traffic in the city was endless and the air quality was poor. She moved to Lyons, Nebraska, and never looked back. "I've got a view of a cornfield, a community where everyone nods a hello when I pass, air that doesn't make me wince. . . . I have everything I need on a daily basis within a very short walk. . . . Honestly, [moving] was not a tough choice," Larsen said.

Nebraska's state capitol building is in Lincoln.

The Omaha Zoo has a large indoor desert and rain forest. To the southwest is Lincoln, Nebraska's capital. It bustles with visitors and residents. Lincoln has museums, a zoo, and large meeting venues. Smaller cities, including Kearny and North Platte, are in the middle of the state.

Nebraska is one of the ten US states that are part of the Great Plains. This region is known for its vast

MAP OF NEBRASKA

Take a look at this map. How does it help you understand the variety of places within Nebraska?

grasslands, rolling hills, and few forests. One remarkable feature in the state is the Sandhills region. This is located in north-central and northwest Nebraska. The Sandhills have grassy valleys and hills that formed over sand dunes.

Most of Nebraska is rural. It has several state and national parks where visitors can learn about Nebraska's unique landforms and history. The parks also feature many native plants and animals. They are great places to explore Nebraska's beauty.

EXPLORE ONLINE

Chapter One discusses Scotts Bluff National Monument. The article at the website below goes into more depth on this topic. Does the article answer any questions you had about the bluff?

SCOTTS BLUFF: GEOLOGIC FEATURES

abdocorelibrary.com/nebraska

Many fossils have been found at Agate Fossil Beds National Monument in Nebraska.

CHAPTER TWO

HISTORY OF NEBRASKA

People have lived in the Nebraska region for thousands of years. The first people came to what is now Nebraska before 8000 BCE. They were nomadic. They relied on bison, so they followed the herds. These people also gathered plants and berries.

By approximately 1000 CE, these people had begun farming the land. Early peoples planted crops. They continued to hunt and fish close to their homes. Eventually the Omaha, Otoe, Pawnee, and Ponca peoples lived in the

Agate Fossil Beds National Monument's museum contains a type of picture calendar by Lakota artist Dawn Little Sky.

central and eastern parts of present-day Nebraska. The Sicangu Lakota Oyate and Oglala Lakota peoples lived in the west. At times, other peoples moved through the western region. These included the Arapaho, Cheyenne, and Comanche (Nʉmʉnʉʉ) peoples.

EUROPEAN AND US EXPLORATION

Spain and France both claimed Nebraska in the late 1600s, even though many American Indians already lived there. The first recorded contact between Europeans and American Indians in Nebraska was in the late 1600s and early 1700s. The Europeans were Spanish and French explorers and fur trappers. They traded objects such as metal tools and glass beads with American Indians. One of the first trading posts in Nebraska was Fort Charles. It was built in 1795 in northeastern Nebraska. Omaha people traded with Europeans there.

In 1800 France gained control of the area that would become Nebraska. Three years later, the

Meriwether Lewis and William Clark boated up the Missouri River, which would later become Nebraska's eastern border.

US government bought this land. It was part of the Louisiana Purchase. The purchase added 530 million acres (214 million ha) of land to the United States. It included parts of what would become 15 US states. US president Thomas Jefferson asked Meriwether Lewis and William Clark to explore the new territory. The explorers' team traveled the lands around the Missouri River starting in 1804.

After Lewis and Clark's expedition, more people came to Nebraska. The area became an important stop for fur traders. Its location along the Missouri River allowed furs from the north and west to travel southward. In the 1840s thousands of white settlers traveled through Nebraska on their way to Utah, California, and Oregon. Some saw opportunities for farming and decided to stay.

FROM TERRITORY TO STATE

The US government officially made Nebraska a territory in 1854. A few years later, the government passed the Homestead Act of 1862. This act provided free land to Americans and people wanting to become Americans. Many people moved to Nebraska. These settlers included immigrants from Germany, Sweden, France, and other European countries.

Around the same time, the US government wanted to build a railroad connecting the East and the West. In 1863 the Central Pacific and Union Pacific railroad companies began construction. The Union Pacific Railroad made its headquarters in Omaha. It started building west from there. Meanwhile the Central Pacific built east from California. The two lines joined in 1869. The longest railroad in the United States was complete.

Nebraska became the thirty-seventh state on March 1, 1867. More and more white settlers came to the area. The increased demand for farmland led to American Indian peoples such as the Ponca being forced from their lands. In the 1870s, the US government made American Indian

PERSPECTIVES
CHIEF RED CLOUD

Chief Red Cloud served as a leader of the Oglala Lakota in Nebraska. In the 1860s the US government began building a road. The road cut through Oglala hunting grounds. Red Cloud wanted to protect his people's land. He led a group of Lakota, Cheyenne, and Arapaho fighters. For two years they attacked workers and stole supplies. Red Cloud refused to stop until the government agreed to end construction. The US government then agreed to quit work on the road.

NEBRASKA QUICK FACTS

Examine these facts and symbols of Nebraska. How do they help you better understand the state?

Abbreviation: NE
Nickname: The Cornhusker State
Motto: Equality before the law
Date of statehood: March 1, 1867
Capital: Lincoln
Population: 1,961,504
Area: 77,348 square miles (200,330 sq km)

STATE SYMBOLS

State bird
Western meadowlark

State flower
Goldenrod

State fish
Channel catfish

State mammal
White-tailed deer

nations such as the Pawnee move to reservations in other states.

Farming continued to grow throughout the late 1800s. But droughts and economic hardships in the 1890s and 1920s helped develop new industries. From 1942 to 1945, Offutt Air Force Base near Omaha made airplanes for World War II (1939–1945). During the war, people began to move from rural areas to cities for new job opportunities.

Omaha's population grew quickly. It was known for its meat-processing industry and livestock markets. In the 1960s Omaha became a center of the civil rights movement. But Nebraska was not done changing. Oil prices began rising in the 1970s and 1980s. While the cost of oil rose, land values fell. The profitable farms were no longer worth as much money as they had been. Nebraskans worked to bring in new businesses and industries, such as manufacturing, at the beginning of the 2000s.

CIVIL RIGHTS

The civil rights movement in the 1950s and 1960s worked to end racial discrimination and segregation in the United States. Many people participated in nonviolent protests. In Omaha, Black people worked hard to stop housing and employment discrimination. They also fought to desegregate public schools.

GOVERNMENT

Nebraska has three branches of government. The legislative branch has only one group of lawmakers, the Senate. Most states have two groups. Nebraska senators vote on bills. Bills that pass go on to the governor. The governor is part of the executive branch and signs bills into law. The third branch is the judicial branch, which consists of a system of courts.

Nebraska also has six recognized American Indian tribes. These are the Iowa Tribe of Kansas and Nebraska, the Omaha Tribe of Nebraska, the Ponca Tribe of Nebraska, the Sac and Fox Nation of Missouri, the Santee Sioux Nation, and the Winnebago Tribe of Nebraska. Each of these tribes has its own government.

STRAIGHT TO THE
SOURCE

During World War II, some German prisoners of war (POWs) were held in camps in Nebraska. Farms were facing labor shortages because men were going off to war. Many prisoners were put to work at places such as farms and canneries. Breanna Fanta of History Nebraska explained how Nebraska brought POWs to farms:

> With agriculture being a primary focus in Nebraska, it was crucial to provide farmers with laborers. In April 1944, the US Department of Agriculture Extension agreed to survey how many prisoners would be needed. Local farm groups were formed to determine this number. Later, the Association for Handling of Negotiations with Army signed contracts with the War Department to employ the prisoners.

Source: Breanna Fanta. "German Prisoners of War in Grand Island." *History Nebraska*, n.d. history.nebraska.gov. Accessed 24 Mar. 2021.

CHANGING MINDS

Take a position on whether or not you support using war prisoners as laborers. Imagine that your best friend has the opposite opinion. Write a short essay trying to change your friend's mind. Make sure you explain your opinion and your reasons for it. Include facts and details that support your reasons.

CHAPTER
THREE

GEOGRAPHY AND CLIMATE

Nebraska lies inside the large Great Plains region. This grassy area stretches across a large chunk of the Midwest. It covers parts of many states, including Texas, Kansas, South Dakota, and North Dakota. Early farmers in Nebraska plowed up much of the grassland to grow crops. But today some places in Nebraska, such as the Glacier Creek Preserve, work to protect areas of grassland. In addition, the Prairie Corridor project aims to connect

Nebraska's Sandhills are full of rolling, grassy hills.

restored prairies in the state. Environmentalists hope this project will allow people to enjoy the tallgrass prairies and recognize the important resources they provide to the state's ecosystem.

Many people think of the Great Plains as flat. But much of the region has rolling hills. The Sandhills are in the northwestern and north-central part of Nebraska. This area is made up of sand dunes that formed approximately 8,000 years ago. Today these dunes are covered in grass. The grass keeps the sand in place. Some of the dunes are 400 feet (120 m) high and 20 miles (32 km) long.

The eastern part of the state is mostly flat. It is not very high above sea level. The rich soil there is good for farming and raising livestock.

A well-known geological landform is in western Nebraska. Chimney Rock is just south of Bayard. This rock formation has a cone-shaped base. A tall spire rises 325 feet (99 m) from the base. Chimney Rock has historical significance too. It was an important landmark for settlers traveling west on the Oregon and California Trails in the 1800s.

WEATHER AND STORMS

Most of Nebraska has similar weather patterns. Summers can be hot. Winters are cold, and the state sometimes gets blizzards. In general, western Nebraska is semiarid. That means this region does not get enough rain to support many plants. The prairie grasses there are short.

PERSPECTIVES

DEVELOPMENT ON SANDHILLS

Some people who live on Nebraska's Sandhills are concerned about big businesses harming the Sandhills ecosystem. Rancher Mel Coffman has spent her life in the Sandhills. She spoke about a power line project that would cut through the area. "The Sandhills are just so precious to me. I feel that as ranchers, our job is to protect and take care of our environment for our livelihood. . . . If you open up the ground, the sand moves. . . . What are the hills going to look like when they get done?" Coffman said.

Eastern Nebraska gets more rainfall and can sustain tallgrass prairies.

Nebraska has an average of 57 tornadoes each year. This is one of the highest tornado counts in the country. Only Texas, Kansas, Florida, and Oklahoma average more per year. Nebraska gets a lot of tornadoes because of its location. Warm and cool air masses meet in Nebraska and form these storms. Most tornadoes in the state happen in the spring and early summer months.

ANIMALS AND PLANTS

Animals and plants have adapted to Nebraska's regions and weather. There are few places to hide from predators in the open plains. Some mammals, such as white-tailed deer and pronghorn, have long legs to help them outrun predators, including wolves and cougars. But overhunting and habitat loss in the late 1800s mostly wiped out these predators from the state. Today there are a few cougars, but wolves are extremely rare

Pronghorn are among the fastest of land animals.

in the state. Other mammals also had to adapt to the open prairie. Some burrow into the soil and form large groups called colonies to survive. These animals include prairie dogs. Prairie dogs use grasses and shrubs for shelter from hawks, weasels, and other predators. Prairies get little rainfall. For this reason, prairie dogs eat plants that have a lot of water in the leaves and roots. This helps the animals survive during droughts.

The Great Plains region is also home to many insects. Beetles, grasshoppers, and locusts feed on the prairie grasses. Some birds, including the western meadowlark and sandhill crane, live in or migrate through the state. Western meadowlarks feast on insects in the tall grasses.

Cottonwoods and elms grow in eastern Nebraska. Pines grow in the central and western regions. The state's prairie grasses are home to a variety of wildflowers that bloom in the spring and summer, such as the goldenrod.

> **WESTERN PRAIRIE FRINGED ORCHID**
>
> The western prairie fringed orchid grows in Nebraska's eastern Sandhills and prairies. But this fragile flower is threatened. Much of the orchid's habitat is now farmland. Mowing and livestock grazing are among the factors that have caused its numbers to drop.

STRAIGHT TO THE SOURCE

Chris Helzer is a prairie ecologist who works as a director at Nebraska's Nature Conservancy. He's also a wildlife photographer. Helzer hopes his work encourages more people to care for prairie ecosystems. He wrote in his book *Hidden Prairie*:

> As a prairie ecologist, writer, and photographer, I spend a lot of time trying to help bring more people into the prairie fold. I want people to recall positive and distinct images when they hear the word "prairie." I want them to have some personal knowledge of the kinds of things that live in prairies. When they read a headline about the destruction of prairies or about threats to their survival, I want them to care. One way to accomplish this is to use engaging photographs that introduce people to the species that live in prairies.

Source: Chris Helzer. *Hidden Prairie*. University of Iowa, 2020, pp. 1–2, books.google.com. Accessed 25 May 2021.

CONSIDER YOUR AUDIENCE

Review the above passage closely. Consider how you would adapt it for a different audience, such as your younger friends. Write a blog post conveying the new information in a way that your friends can understand. How does your new approach differ from the original text, and why?

CHAPTER FOUR

RESOURCES AND ECONOMY

Nebraska's vast prairies mean that agriculture is an important industry within the state. Ten percent of the population works in agriculture. In 2020 Nebraska farmers produced more than $7 billion worth of corn and grain. Farmers also grow alfalfa, hay, wheat, soybeans, dry beans, and sorghum. The state is known for livestock farms too. These farms raise large numbers of hogs, as well as cattle, poultry, and sheep.

Some farms in Nebraska grow corn.

PERSPECTIVES
JOINING THE FARMING INDUSTRY

In 2020 Zemua Baptista became a first-generation farmer, which was his lifelong dream. "I just always knew I wanted to be a farmer. It's always been what I grew up around," he said. As a young adult, Baptista earned a college degree in agricultural economics while also forming a business plan to become a poultry farmer. He built eight barns near Seward, Nebraska, to raise broiler chicks. Baptista is one of the few Black farmers in the state. In 2017 only 22 of Nebraska's more than 77,000 farmers were Black.

The number of farms is decreasing within the state. In 1934 Nebraska had approximately 135,000 farms. In the early 2000s, that number dropped to 50,000. However, the remaining farms are larger than those of the past. In 1965 the average farm was less than 600 acres (240 ha). That average increased to 930 acres (376 ha) in the early 2000s.

Nebraska has worked to make its economy diverse. Manufacturing is important to the state. Many of these businesses, such as machine and chemical plants, are

Shown here in 1973, Interstate 80 runs east to west across Nebraska. It has been an important route through the state for decades.

found in large cities. The state is also known for its food processing industry.

Transportation is also important to Nebraska's economy. Many interstate highways cross the state. This makes Nebraska a popular route for transporting goods to other parts of the country. Major railroads also cut through the state, including through Lincoln and

Omaha. In addition, Omaha is a port city because of its location on the Missouri River. Commercial barges carry products up and down the river.

ENERGY

Nebraska produces some forms of renewable energy. This energy comes from sources that replenish naturally, such as sun, wind, and plants. Biofuels are renewable. Nebraska is one of the top producers of biofuels. Biofuels are energy sources that come from plant or animal materials. One type of biofuel is called ethanol. It's made from corn. Ethanol can replace oil-based fuels. Much of this

WIND POWER

About 19 percent of Nebraska's energy generation comes from wind power. The Nebraska Department of Labor notes that Nebraskans have been using wind power since the early settler days, when windmills pumped water from wells. In 2019 wind power was a growing energy source. That year, Nebraska had more than 970 wind turbines. Hundreds of people worked in the industry, and the number was expected to rise.

product is made in rural communities. Nebraska is the second-largest producer of ethanol in the United States. Thousands of Nebraskans have jobs in this industry.

Nebraska uses other renewable energy sources too. The state's large, wind-swept plains are dotted with wind turbines. These huge machines harness wind to produce power. In addition, Nebraska's large rivers are natural sources of hydropower, which captures energy from moving water.

FURTHER EVIDENCE

Chapter Four discusses biofuel in Nebraska. Identify one of the author's main points. What evidence does the author provide to support this point? The article at the website below also discusses the topic. Find a quote in this article that supports the author's main point. Does it offer a new piece of evidence?

BIOFUELS. EXPLAINED
abdocorelibrary.com/nebraska

CHAPTER FIVE

PEOPLE AND PLACES

Nebraska is a mix of big cities and rural towns. Approximately 90 percent of the state is farmland. However, nearly 75 percent of Nebraskans live in cities. Most of the population is white. Many people have European ancestry, including Czech, German, and Irish heritages. But approximately 7 percent of the population was born outside of the United States. Many of these people are from Mexico. They came to Nebraska to work in agriculture and in the

People in Nebraska sometimes hold festivals to celebrate their heritages, such as Czech heritage.

many meatpacking plants. Black people are about 5 percent of the population. Nearly 3 percent of Nebraskans are Asian.

American Indian people continue to live in Nebraska. They make up 1.5 percent of the population. Some live on reservations. The Santee Sioux Nation has a reservation near Niobrara, Nebraska. The Winnebago Tribe of Nebraska has a reservation in Winnebago. The Omaha Tribe of Nebraska has a reservation that borders the Winnebago reservation. Approximately one-third of Nebraska's American Indian people live in large cities such as Omaha and Lincoln.

FAMOUS NEBRASKANS

A number of famous people come from Nebraska. Nicholas Sparks is a well-known author who was born in Omaha. He's written books such as *The Notebook*, *A Walk to Remember*, and *The Last Song*. Many of his books have been made into movies.

Hilary Swank was born in Lincoln and has twice won the Academy Award for Best Actress. Clayton C. Anderson is a former NASA astronaut. He was born in Omaha and grew up in Ashland. He spent a total of 167 days in space across his missions.

EVENTS AND SIGHTS

American Indian traditions are honored in the state. American Indian peoples hold powwows each year. These events celebrate a nation's history and heritage. For instance,

PERSPECTIVES
MALCOLM X

Malcolm X was an influential figure during the 1950s and 1960s civil rights movement. He was born Malcolm Little in Omaha in 1925. As an adult, he changed his last name. Malcolm X spoke on the streets of Harlem, New York, as well as at respected colleges such as the University of Oxford and Harvard University. He criticized US society for how it treated Black people. Malcolm X had many ideas on how to achieve Black racial independence. In contrast to Dr. Martin Luther King Jr.'s tactic of nonviolent protests, Malcolm X encouraged people to protect themselves "by any means necessary."

The Winnebago Tribe of Nebraska is among those that hold powwows.

the Omaha Tribe of Nebraska holds a harvest powwow each August. This tradition has been going on for more than 200 years. Celebrations include dancing, singing, and sharing traditional foods. The event takes place over a few days, and everyone is welcome to join the celebration.

The Czech Festival is another popular event in Nebraska. It takes place in Wilber and highlights the eastern European influences in the state. Some people wear traditional Czech clothes. The festival has many events, including a tractor pull, a Czech heritage demonstration, an accordion jamboree, an art show, and a parade.

For people looking for outdoor adventures, Nebraska has many state parks. The state's warm, sunny summers are good for hiking. Cross-country skiers take advantage of groomed trails in the winter. Whether in the city or on the trail, Nebraska is full of adventure.

HUSKER FOOTBALL

College football is a Nebraska tradition. The University of Nebraska's college football team, the Cornhuskers, played its first game in 1890. From then on, the team was a powerhouse. Many talented coaches and athletes came through Nebraska. One of the most famous players was Johnny Rodgers, a wide receiver. In 1970 and 1971, he led the Huskers to two national championships. Quick on his feet, Rodgers could turn catches into touchdowns. Rodgers was Nebraska's first Heisman Trophy winner in 1972.

IMPORTANT DATES

8000 BCE
Nomadic people follow bison herds through what has become modern-day Nebraska.

1000 CE
People begin farming the land in the Nebraska area.

1600s
France and Spain both claim Nebraska.

1795
The Fort Charles trading post is built in Nebraska, allowing Omaha people and Europeans to trade goods.

1803
Nebraska becomes part of the United States in the Louisiana Purchase.

1867
Nebraska becomes the thirty-seventh state on March 1.

1869
The first US transcontinental railroad, which cuts through Nebraska, is completed.

1942–1945
Offutt Air Force Base builds airplanes for World War II.

2000s
Fewer people own farms in the state, but the farms that remain are larger.

STOP AND THINK

Surprise Me
Chapter Five discusses people and places in Nebraska. After reading this chapter, what two or three facts about Nebraska did you find most surprising? Write a few sentences about each fact. Why did you find each fact surprising?

Say What?
Studying states can mean learning a lot of new vocabulary. Find five words in this book you've never heard before. Use a dictionary to find out what they mean. Then write the meanings in your own words and use each word in a new sentence.

Take a Stand
Some people want to develop parts of Nebraska's natural land, such as the Sandhills, for businesses. Others want to keep the land natural. Do you think it's more important for people to use land for income or to protect natural landscapes? Or do you think a balance between the two is most important? Explain your answer.

You Are There

Chapter Three discusses geography, plants, and wildlife in Nebraska. Imagine you are traveling to the state. Write a letter home telling your friends what you see. What do you notice about the different kinds of land? What animals live in each place? Be sure to add plenty of detail to your notes.

GLOSSARY

adapt
to change over time to develop a feature or skill that helps an animal or plant survive

diverse
having a lot of variety

drought
a long period of little or no rain

heritage
cultural history or background that is passed down through families and communities

nomadic
having no set home but traveling from place to place, often with the seasons to find food

reservation
an area of land set aside for American Indian people

rural
having to do with the countryside

tactic
a strategy or method of achieving a goal

ONLINE RESOURCES

To learn more about Nebraska, visit our free resource websites below.

Visit **abdocorelibrary.com** or scan this QR code for free Common Core resources for teachers and students, including vetted activities, multimedia, and booklinks, for deeper subject comprehension.

Visit **abdobooklinks.com** or scan this QR code for free additional online weblinks for further learning. These links are routinely monitored and updated to provide the most current information available.

LEARN MORE

Cooper, Robert. *Nebraska Cornhuskers*. Abdo, 2021.

Gagne, Tammy. *Exploring the Midwest*. Abdo, 2018.

Smith, Sherri L. *What Is the Civil Rights Movement?* Penguin, 2020.

INDEX

agriculture, 6, 13, 16–19, 21, 23–24, 28, 31–32, 37
American Indians, 6, 13–14, 17–20, 38–40

bison, 6, 13

Chief Red Cloud, 17
Chimney Rock, 9, 24
civil rights, 19, 20, 39
Cornhusker State, 6, 18

Europeans, 14, 16, 37, 40–41

famous people, 38–39

government, 5, 15–17, 20

Great Plains, 8, 23–24, 28

insects, 28

Jefferson, Thomas, 15

Lewis and Clark, 15
Lincoln, 8, 9, 18, 33, 38–39
Louisiana Purchase, 15

manufacturing, 19, 32–33
Missouri River, 7, 9, 15–16, 34

Omaha, 7–8, 9, 16, 19, 20, 34, 38–39

Platte River, 7, 9
prairie dogs, 27
prairies, 5–6, 23–28, 29, 31

railroads, 16–17, 33
renewable energy, 34–35

Sandhills, 11, 24, 25, 28
Scotts Bluff National Monument, 5, 6, 9, 11

tornadoes, 26

western prairie fringed orchid, 28
white-tailed deer, 18, 26

About the Author

Lynn Ternus is a children's book writer who lives in northern Minnesota.